Original title:
Moss and Musings

Copyright © 2025 Creative Arts Management OÜ
All rights reserved.

Author: Amelia Montgomery
ISBN HARDBACK: 978-1-80567-166-4
ISBN PAPERBACK: 978-1-80567-465-8

Grounded in Green

In the garden, green things sprout,
Wiggly worms dance about.
Rabbits hop, they lay the law,
While squirrels plot without a flaw.

Leaves gossip with the passing breeze,
Tickling toes with playful tease.
Frogs hop round in a grand parade,
While shadows play, a little charade.

Whispers of the Woodland

In the woods, the trees conspire,
Squirrels scamper, never tire.
Birds crack jokes in their fine nests,
While the fox plays at being the best.

A rabbit snickers at a shy deer,
'You call that running? Have no fear!'
Leaves snicker while they slowly turn,
As the sunlight makes the branches burn.

The Soliloquy of Sublime Silence

A deer doth ponder where snacks reside,
While wise old owls smirk with pride.
The brook chuckles, flows with ease,
Stirring giggles from the trees.

Mushrooms lounge, sporting caps so bright,
Sharing secrets of day and night.
Every rustle, a punchline's birth,
Nature's jesters share their mirth.

Notes from the Glistening Realm

Beneath the ferns, a beetle sings,
About the joys that splashing brings.
Raindrops laugh, they tumble down,
Each one dressed in a sparkling crown.

Wet stones chuckle as they sit,
Reminding all to just admit.
That in the puddles, dance of light,
Every splash is pure delight.

Voices Among the Verdure

In the woods, the trees conspire,
Squirrels gossip, fuel their fire.
Leaves chuckle as they twist and twirl,
Frogs joke about the odd girl.

Birds chirp their jokes without a care,
Rabbits giggle, fluff their hair.
Under each old, gnarled root,
Laughter echoes, wild and cute.

A Tapestry of Gentle Thoughts

A snail slithered, took his time,
While crickets chirped in perfect rhyme.
Each step left a trail of cheer,
'Just keep it slow,' was his advice clear.

The flowers swayed in gentle tease,
Flirting with the buzzing bees.
One whispered, 'Do you think I'm bright?'
'Then shine on, darling, soft and light!'

Whispers Beneath the Canopy

Under branches, shadows dance,
Mice throw a wild, tiny prance.
They whisper secrets in the shade,
Of cheese and crumbs that never fade.

A raccoon waves with a sly wink,
Nature's shenanigans in sync.
Leaves rustle, giggles take flight,
A mischievous fawn steals the night.

Lichen's Lullaby

On the rock, a culture thrives,
Lichens sing while nature jives.
Their voices soft, a cozy hum,
Beneath the moon, they strum and strum.

The whispers trap the passing breeze,
Winking at the calm, tall trees.
Every sound a playful sigh,
As sleepy stars begin to fly.

Stories Steeped in Shade

Under ferns, the secrets thrive,
Whispers of the forest jive.
Squirrels giggle, shadows play,
Fables sprout in bright array.

Worms in bow ties strut around,
In their world, they're quite renowned.
Snails race fast at their own pace,
Every slow-meeting's a wild chase.

The Art of Being Still

A boulder sits, it feels so proud,
Crickets chirp a quirky crowd.
The sun beams down, a lazy gaze,
Nature's comic in a daze.

Turtles pose in perfect grace,
Stretching slow in their own space.
While every leaf brings laughter's cheer,
Time stands still, oh isn't it queer?

Ethereal Shades of Earth

In twilight's glow, the mushrooms wink,
A friendly glow, or so we think.
Fairies giggle, ninjas peek,
Underfoot, a sneaky creek.

Leafy hats for bugs so spry,
Dance on air as raindrops sigh.
A rabbit dressed in velvet shoes,
Prances round, with nothing to lose.

Interlude in the Understory

A hedgehog hums a silly tune,
While fireflies start to swoon at noon.
The breeze does wiggles, soft and sly,
As butterflies dance, oh my, oh my!

Under limbs where shadows meet,
A festival of smells and feet.
The earth spins laughter, wild and free,
Join the chorus of jubilee!

The Quietude of Enchanted Groves

In the shade where whispers play,
Squirrels giggle, then run away.
Trees wear hats of leafy grace,
While mushrooms hide, a funny face.

Sunlight dances, a jolly jig,
Bugs hold parties, oh so big!
A frog croaks jokes from his wet stone,
While butterflies flutter, never alone.

Winds sing softly, a cheerful tune,
Telling secrets of sun and moon.
Branches bend with laughter, true,
As shadows waltz in an emerald hue.

Here in the grove, time dares not peek,
Nature chuckles, her humor unique.
Where silence reigns and jesters prance,
Each leafy laugh sparks a joyful dance.

Memories Woven in Foliage

Leaves remember stories dear,
Of clumsy falls and silly cheer.
A raccoon's laugh, a rabbit's hop,
Echoes of joy that never stop.

A vine swings low, a friendly tease,
While ants march in their tiny breeze.
Forgotten shoes, a child's delight,
Retold in whispers, day and night.

Mushrooms giggle, what a sight!
A deer trips over in sheer fright.
Nature's scrapbook, crammed with mirth,
Retells the tales of playful worth.

Breezy gigs from trees so tall,
Life's tiny marvels make us enthrall.
A tapestry rich, in greens, we see,
Memories laugh as they sway carefree.

Sheltered by Nature's Embrace

Underneath a leafy dome,
Creatures frolic, making home.
A snail slips by with an empty grin,
Wishing for speed, but stuck within.

Icicles laugh as they dangle low,
Taunting the flowers that want to grow.
A spider spins tales of wobbly grace,
Fridays are silly in this leafy place.

Toads tell tales that echo wide,
Of awkward dances, and bug pride.
Fairies giggle, hiding behind
Petals that remain blissfully unconfined.

Here laughter lives, it won't erase,
As critters bounce in this warm embrace.
Nature's corners are sprinkled with fun,
Just step inside—let the jokes be spun.

Ponderings in the Green Abyss

In the deep where shadows play,
Goblins grumble, then sway away.
Thorns whisper secrets, tales of old,
Of squirrels with courage, far too bold.

A tree stump wears a wise old frown,
While a wandering snail slides down.
Questions bob upon the breeze,
As chirps arise from cheeky bees.

Nature's chat, a silly tease,
What's the hurry? Just take it easy!
Fungi wear spectacles, wise and round,
Their laughter swirling through the ground.

In this abyss, thoughts twist and weave,
All the wonders that we believe.
So come my friends, let's laugh and share,
For in this grove, joy fills the air.

Whimsical Writings on the Forest Floor

In a world of leaves, I ponder,
Where acorns plot their next great blunder.
Squirrels giggle at my plight,
While ants dance near, oh what a sight!

Frogs croak secrets, bold and brash,
While chipmunks laugh in a lightning flash.
The twigs are pens; the ground, my page,
Each creature joins the woodland Stage!

Pine cones testify of lost romance,
While wildflowers strike a silly stance.
Laughter echoes through the trees,
As nature feasts on witty leaves.

I write a story, just for fun,
Among the critters, everyone.
A symphony of chuckles, bright,
Nature's comedy, pure delight!

Dreaming in the Dappled Sun

Sunbeams dance like playful sprites,
While bees compete in silly flights.
A butterfly flirts, as if to tease,
While shadows chuckle upon the trees.

The breeze whispers jokes, soft and sweet,
Beneath the branches, soft and neat.
A ladybug dons a tiny crown,
And to my laughter, it won't back down.

The forest floor is a cushion to lay,
As I dream of pickles on a sunny day.
The mushrooms giggle, wearing their hats,
Turning my thoughts to jovial chats.

With sun-kissed giggles in my head,
The woodland winks as clouds turn red.
This dappled comfort, filled with fun,
In nature's embrace, I feel like a bun!

Carvings of Time in Nature's Palate

Trees compose a long, tall chat,
About the squirrels and where they sat.
With every ring, a tale unfolds,
Of mischief and secrets that never get old.

The stones chuckle, smooth and round,
At the gossip of the critters found.
While twigs and leaves craft stories bright,
Of tiny adventures that beam with light.

In each hollow, a narrative spins,
Of feasts and brawls where nature grins.
The laughter of grass, a rustling tune,
Plays under the watchful eye of the moon.

Each carving whispers from the past,
With memories and giggles that always last.
The forest gallery, humor in sight,
Stories abound, an endless delight!

The Spirit of Growth and Stillness

Beneath the stillness, laughter brews,
As plants share jokes and silly views.
A sprout declares, 'I'm quite the star!'
While a snail says, 'I'll get there, just afar.'

The ferns all sway with giddy glee,
As the daisies toss down tea with glee.
Roots entwine, a playful scheme,
To tickle the toes of those who dream.

The air is thick with giggles and grins,
As whispers of growth lead to silly spins.
A wise old oak chuckles thick and deep,
While nature's lullabies coax us to sleep.

In every corner, laughter grows,
While wonders bloom where no one knows.
A spirit of joy in every glance,
As life reveals its charming dance!

Beneath the Veil of Life

In shady patches, there they lie,
Little green carpets, oh my, oh my!
They watch the world pass, they giggle and grin,
With secrets tucked under their fluffy skin.

With a poke and a prod, they dance in delight,
Hiding the crickets who party all night.
The squirrels roll their eyes, what a sight to see,
Nature's own jesters, as jolly as can be.

A raindrop arrives, a slippery friend,
Turns all the fungi to play 'pretend.'
"Let's become umbrellas!" the toadstools all cheer,
While ants in tuxedos appear with a beer.

So wander along where the sunlight fades,
In patches of laughter, where joy cascades.
Life underneath seems to flourish and thrive,
In the humor of nature, we're truly alive.

Nature's Poetic Palette

In splashes of green on the forest floor,
There's a flurry of jokes behind every door.
The gnomes in the garden, with smiles so wide,
Trade puns with the weeds, such a merry ride.

A ladybug ponders the flea's crazy ways,
"It's easier up here, I just sunbathe all days!"
While butterflies giggle, they flit to and fro,
Making up tales about where they will go.

"Who wore it better?" two flowers debate,
While the mushrooms insist they'll just have to wait.
The briars all whisper about last week's fun,
A mustache on the snail had them on the run!

So if you should wander through shades close and light,
Be mindful of laughter, for nature's polite.
In every soft whisper and rustle you hear,
The universe chuckles, so lend it an ear.

The Understory Chronicles

Down low in the brush where the shadows may creep,
Lies a tale of the critters who never sleep.
A rabbit tells stories as the fireflies wink,
While explaining to turtles why they're always pink.

The hedgehogs are giggling at last week's great race,
While giggly grasshoppers stretch out in their space.
"I hopped over the puddle!" a frog does exclaim,
But no one quite believes him, it's all just a game.

A warbler sings loudly of the wind's funny twists,
While a wise old worm offers some comedic twists.
"Why fight against fate? Just wiggle away,
Dance out of the shadows, enjoy every day!"

In this lively underworld where laughter's the way,
Every leaf tells a story, every twig wants to play.
So cherish the whispers beneath the tall trees,
Where humor's the nectar that sways in the breeze.

Silent Sentinels of the Woods

Beneath the tall giants with faces of bark,
The quiet observers lie waiting till dark.
Not a sound escapes, just a chuckle or two,
As they watch all the hikers trip over a shoe.

The ferns share a secret, they flutter and sway,
"Did you hear what she said? No way, not today!"
The mushrooms all giggle, "We're feeling so bright!
Let's throw a surprise party—who'll dance through the night?"

"Beware of the humans!" the raccoons declare,
"Last week they just wandered right into our lair!"
The stumps all are chatting, exchanging old jokes,
As the crickets provide a comedic folk song.

So stroll through the forest, discover the cheer,
In the company of silliness, nature's so near.
For among the tall sentinels, glee fills the air,
While laughter reminds us life's truly quite rare.

The Texture of Tranquility

A soft carpet sprawls, so green,
It cushions every little scene.
Frogs croak jokes at the break of dawn,
Mocking the bugs that get it wrong.

Twirling leaves dance in the breeze,
Whispering secrets of the trees.
Squirrels giggle, gathering treats,
Like clowns on quest for tasty feats.

A cat on a branch, just hangs around,
Laughing at friends who touch the ground.
With each step, a crunch, a squish,
Life's silly humor is the sweetest dish.

Beneath the layers, laughter stirs,
Tranquil sighs and playful purrs.
Nature's jesters, bright and bold,
In this soft world, we are consoled.

Secrets of the Understory

In the shade where shadows play,
Whispers prance in a leafy ballet.
Rabbits giggle beneath the fronds,
While ants embark on grand absconds.

Slugs slide past with a regal flair,
Claiming thrones in the cool, damp air.
Chasing sunshine is quite the sport,
As butterflies hold their own report.

Pine cones tumble, a silent cheer,
As critters gather, drawing near.
Beneath the ferny, fragile dome,
They share the tales of a secret home.

In twinkling trails, old stories light,
Of hopping hares and mice in flight.
The underbrush crackles, laughter roars,
In this hidden world, the fun just soars.

Ruminations in the Thicket's Heart

In the depths where shadows creep,
Thoughts collide and laughter leaps.
A hedgehog's grin, so shy yet wise,
Mocks the moss with gleaming eyes.

Through tangled vines and playful bows,
Imagination twirls and bows.
Turtles ponder, slow and grand,
Dreaming of steals from nature's hand.

Wisdom lies in the crooked bark,
Hints of joy in each tiny spark.
Bramble whispers, "Come take a seat,"
As the world giggles softly beneath our feet.

Among the roots, we count our dreams,
In this thicket, laughter teems.
Rambling whimsies take their flight,
In this heart of hush, our time is bright.

Timeless Patina of the Forest Path

Footsteps echo on the trail,
Silly squirrels tell their tale.
Echos of laughter blend with leaves,
As the forest hums and weaves.

Old stones smirk, adorned with age,
As if life's folly comes from stage.
Each twist and turn, a new surprise,
Nature winks with knowing eyes.

Dirt-strewn laughter clings to air,
In harmony, we lose our care.
Crickets chirp a comical tune,
As the sun dips low, our spirits balloon.

Timeless paths lead us around,
Where every nook holds joy profound.
In nature's arms, we spin and dance,
For here, how silly is our chance!

The Class of Composition

In a classroom dim and bright,
Pens a-dancing, words take flight.
Paper planes that never soar,
Teachers sigh, they want much more.

Jokes scribbled in the margins wide,
Sentences that slip and slide.
Paragraphs with wiggles, prance,
The grammar rules don't stand a chance!

Assignments due, with chaos rife,
Mixing metaphors like stir-fried life.
Each typo a reason to chuckle,
The red pen rides in for the buckle!

So here's to drafts that miss the mark,
And essays that just fizz and spark.
We laugh and learn, we write and rhyme,
Composing chaos, one line at a time.

Leaves of Reflection

A leaf falls down, a clumsy dance,
Nature's way of taking a chance.
It spins and twirls, a dizzy show,
"Catch me," it whispers, "if you know!"

In puddles deep, reflections tease,
Frogs jump in with grace and ease.
Water droplets, a vibrant splash,
Rippling stories, secrets clash.

Amidst the chaos, birds remark,
"Is that a leaf or just a lark?"
With every breeze, they flit and glide,
In laughter's breeze, the leaf can't hide!

So when you see a leaf's parade,
Join the fun, don't be afraid.
For nature spins its funny tale,
In every green and golden trail.

Intertwined in the Inconspicuous

In shadows faint, where whispers grow,
Two squirrels argue, a lively show.
"Your nuts are mine!" the chatter rings,
Life's little drama, just like kings.

Among the weeds, a secret pact,
A toad and rat make quite the act.
Gossip flies, each tail a flail,
As they spin tales, a funny gale.

A flower peeks, its petals shy,
Facepalming leaves as clouds pass by.
"Can we not talk? Let's just bloom!"
In this odd plot, they share the room.

So when you wander, look around,
In every corner, laughter's found.
The inconspicuous hum of glee,
Nature's jesters, wild and free!

The Subtle Story Weavers

In quiet corners, tales unspool,
Two spiders crafting, crafty and cool.
"Did you hear?" one silkily spun,
"Last night I caught a fly for fun!"

The other giggles, "Oh, what luck!
My web's a lounge, come take a pluck!"
They weave their webs with threads of cheer,
Secrets spun, for all to hear.

A ladybug strolls, dapper and bright,
"Good day, dear friends, what's the delight?"
With laughs exchanged, they spin their yarns,
Weaving joy in nature's charms.

So take a moment, watch them play,
In subtle stories, night and day.
For life is rich, with threads anew,
In every corner, joy shines through.

The Softness of the Forgotten

In shadows low, the green does creep,
A couch for critters, where dreams do leap.
With whispers soft, they gently sway,
In secrets known, they dance and play.

Did you know that slugs like to slide?
On plushy beds, they take their ride.
With laughter echoing on the ground,
Beneath their joys, a world profound.

The ants parade, all dressed in cheer,
In this lush land, they have no fear.
With tiny hats and tiny shoes,
They host a bash, you can't refuse!

So next you stroll, look down with glee,
At patches soft, where wonders flee.
It's not just dirt, it's a delight,
Where life's peculiar, and laughs are bright.

Hidden Realms of the Overlooked

In corners dim, where sunlight wanes,
Life blooms beneath, in silly veins.
A kingdom thrives, not found in books,
With gnomes and fairies, and cheeky looks.

The beetle struts with dazzling flair,
Curbing the sassy chipmunk's stare.
In every nook, the giggles rise,
A treasure trove that mocks the skies.

Dandelion crowns on the lil' ones' heads,
As tiny dreams float like soft-spun threads.
In laughter shared, a secret plays,
In hidden realms, where wild hearts gaze.

So take a glance and look real close,
At all the antics in quiet prose.
For life can jest in softest sheen,
In worlds that lie where few have been.

A Tapestry of Tiny Worlds

Underfoot lies a vibrant quilt,
Stitched with laughter and gleeful guilt.
Each patch a tale, so small yet grand,
With tiny sprites lending a hand.

The ladybugs wear polka dot suits,
As butterflies play on tiny flutes.
The beetles build, with playful glee,
While you just wonder, 'What's this spree?'

A curious snail surveys the land,
With dreams so big, yet life so planned.
Its shell a home, a mother ship,
That sails through muck on a slippery trip.

So pause for fun in the grassy expanse,
Where all that crawls partakes in dance.
For in small things, laughter spins,
A tapestry where joy begins.

When the Ground Speaks

Listen close to what lies beneath,
The tales of dirt, the stories sheathed.
With gentle sighs, the earth will share,
The gossip of roots, if you just dare.

A worm tells jokes as it wiggles on,
While crickets join in, until the dawn.
A chorus of chuckles, rich and bright,
With each hidden twist bringing pure delight.

The rocks keep secrets, ancient and wise,
In cracked old faces, a glint of surprise.
With each rattle echoing from the ground,
The laughter bubbles, it knows no bound.

So kneel awhile, and lend your ear,
To whispers soft, and quirky cheer.
For when the earth begins to speak,
You'll find the funny in every peak.

Growth in Glistening Silence

In corners where the shadows blend,
A carpet grows without a friend.
It giggles softly at my shoes,
Whispers secrets, leaves no clues.

A tiny kingdom underfoot,
Where little critters dare to scoot.
Each dew drop giggles as it clings,
To slyly tiptoe while it sings.

Roots twist in laughter, all around,
In this realm, joy is unbound.
A dance of greens, a wobbly spree,
Oh, what a silly sight to see!

When I stop to have a peek,
Those little wonders start to squeak.
A punchline hidden in each sprout,
Nature's jesters, without a doubt.

The Beneath That Breathes

Down below where no one dares,
Life's laughter echoes, none declares.
With pulsating rhythm, roots do sway,
Who knew the underground could play?

Wiggly worms with silly dreams,
Plotting pranks, or so it seems.
A gnome pops out to say hello,
"Join in the fun! Come on, let's go!"

Laughter bubbles in the earth,
Each creature sings of hidden mirth.
A party hosted by the weeds,
Where nonsense grows from tiny seeds.

It's a gala for the unseen crew,
Where every shade of green's in view.
If you should listen, you might hear,
The silly giggles drawing near.

Thoughts in the Underbrush

In tangled thoughts where rabbits roam,
I find my way just like a gnome.
Fuzzy ideas start to sprout,
Nonsensical—their code, no doubt.

A ladybug takes flight with flair,
Dances about without a care.
With tiny claps, she sets the scene,
Unruly dreams in shades of green.

The whispers rustle through the leaves,
As playful tricksters tease and weave.
Each rustling branch unveils a joke,
A giggle here, a chuckle broke.

So when you walk through thicket's maze,
Remember all the merry ways.
The thoughts that lurk in secret paths,
Are sneaky voices, full of laughs.

Tread Softly

Tread softly here, watch where you go,
The ground beneath has tales to show.
With every step, the soil sighs,
As creatures wink with tiny eyes.

Pinecones chuckle at my feet,
Old leaves gossip in rhythm sweet.
A scurry from beneath the brush,
What secrets hide within that hush?

A dandelion tips its head,
With wishes whispering, unspread.
Beware the puns the grass will write,
For laughter hides where it's polite.

So tiptoe lightly, peer around,
The world below is lushly found.
Among the giggles, quick, take heed,
For nature's jesters plant their seed.

Nature's Narrative

In every grove, a tale to tell,
Stories spun from the soil's dwell.
A voice of nature, bold and brash,
Crafts clever jokes with a little flash.

The spider spins a web of jest,
Each silken strand, a daring quest.
With every twitch, the humor swells,
In leafy paths where mirth compels.

A toad croaks out a punchline bright,
While shadows dance in fading light.
Each evening's curtain is drawn tight,
When laughter bubbles, pure delight.

So stroll along this quirky scene,
Where humor lurks among the green.
Listen close, the wild will say,
That life's a joke in a funny way.

Relics of Earthly Elegance

In the whispers of the ground,
Fungi dance without a sound,
Wearing hats both bright and bold,
Secrets of the earth unfold.

Tiny creatures roam with glee,
Waging wars for bits of debris,
Their kingdom thrives, a playful spree,
Who knew dirt could hold such glee?

Twisting roots weave tales untold,
Of fuzzy socks and stories old,
With every wiggle, every grin,
The humor lies within the skin.

When rain arrives, they slip and slide,
On nature's stage, they love to glide,
In puddles deep, they jump about,
Who knew the ground had such a clout?

Sables of the Subtle

In shadows where the critters creep,
Soft blankets form where secrets seep,
Crickets chirp in jest, so spry,
Underneath a giggling sky.

A squirrel pulls its finest threads,
To weave a cap atop its heads,
While snails race slow, with no despair,
In their grand pace, they find their flair.

The softest hues of green abound,
As kittens take to twisting ground,
They tumble, trip, then pounce again,
Laughing off their soft disdain.

In this realm of sneaky fun,
Where every creature's on the run,
Nature chuckles, can't resist,
A comedy we can't dismiss.

Nature's Hidden Threads

Beneath the thicket's tangled fests,
The grass confesses silly quests,
With ants that march in perfect lines,
Together plotting grand designs.

The daisies bloom, don hats so fly,
While butterflies and bees pass by,
"Excuse me!" says a ladybug,
"You block my view, you fuzzy mug!"

The wind joins in, with playful swirls,
Spreading giggles among the curls,
As petals dance in breezy cheer,
A witty world that's ever near.

Each layer hides a joke or two,
From wormy thoughts to clover's view,
Nature laughs, a merry sound,
In every corner, joy is found.

Beneath the Green Canopy

Beneath the leaves, a trickster plays,
With shadows cast in funny ways,
A raccoon dons a leafy crown,
As squirrels laugh and spin around.

The grasshoppers break into a show,
With leaps that steal the very glow,
They chirp a tune of pure delight,
A folly wrapped in greenish light.

The roots, they whisper jokes galore,
Like tales of what was found before,
In every nook, a pun awaits,
An earthy laugh within the straits.

So take a breath, let laughter flow,
In nature's realms, a fun tableau,
Amid the green, let spirits lift,
With every giggle, find your gift.

Vitamin D and Decomposed Dreams

Sipping sun beams, I took a leap,
Chasing warmth while the squirrels sleep.
A dance with shadows, I prance around,
In my cozy nest, I'm glory-bound.

Bread crumbs scattered turn to gold,
Laughter echoes, adventures unfold.
Decomposed dreams beneath my feet,
Who knew that fungi could be a treat?

Down the rabbit hole, I took a chance,
Fell on my face, but gave it a dance.
Rambunctious thoughts in the bright sunlight,
Decomposed laughter is pure delight!

Climbing ladders leads to who knows where,
Finding treasures under the stair.
So I'll keep leaping into the fray,
With Vitamin D lighting my way!

The Quiet Nurturers

In corners quiet, whispers grow,
Tickling roots, beneath the show.
A shuffle of leaves, a giggle or two,
Nature's secret, hidden from view.

Gentle guardians cradle the ground,
In their stillness, laughter is found.
They wiggle and wobble without a care,
With all that tittering, they must beware!

Who knew the soil could be so sly?
Deeds of the dusk that peek and pry.
With each little sprig, a story is spun,
From seeds of the past, we all can have fun.

Roots plunge deep as giggles fly,
Misty mornings, a joyful sigh.
So raise a toast with me, my friend,
To those quiet nurturers that never end!

Beneath the Ancient Trees

Under the giants, I doze and dream,
Tickling trifles dance through the beam.
Branches whisper secrets they hold dear,
While I giggle, lost in 'what's over here?'

Nutty neighbors throw their jests,
"Oh look! A twirl!" my mind contests.
With every rustle, laughter takes flight,
A congregation of whimsy at night.

Beneath the verdant, tangled embrace,
Joy unspools in this happy place.
The wise old trunks might chuckle slow,
As tiny creatures put on a show.

Leaves flutter gently in a slight breeze,
It's a symposium of giggles, if you please.
So here's to the stories that roots can share,
Beneath the ancient trees, we breathe the air!

Cascades of Time and Texture

Time trickles like a playful stream,
Each droplet dances, chasing a dream.
Fuzzy textures weave tales untold,
Underfoot carpets of emerald gold.

Silly snapshots stuck in the bark,
Where do they hide when it gets dark?
With a wink and a wiggle, they share their tales,
Of wild wind chases and long-lost trails.

Curled up shadows form cozy beds,
While mossy mischief fills our heads.
A timbre of laughter echoes anew,
As we chase down giggles where wild things grew.

So come take a stroll, don't mind the clocks,
In this tapestry where whimsy unlocks.
Cascades of joy in each squishy step,
Laughter and magic, our hearts adept!

Fragments of Forgotten Fronds

In a patch where shadows creep,
Ferns giggle secrets they keep.
A toadstool winks with delight,
While snails take their leisurely flight.

A squirrel sips dew from a cap,
As the world takes a cozy nap.
The air is thick with glee and cheer,
Nature's jokes are loud and clear.

Bumblebees dance with such flair,
Doing the cha-cha with the air.
A dandelion says, "Look at me!"
As the wind blows wild and free.

In this garden of endless delight,
Laughter echoes, both day and night.
Each leaf a storyteller bold,
Whispering tales of humor untold.

Veils of Verdant Wonder

Underneath a leafy cloak,
Lies a world of silly folk.
Pixies hide behind the stems,
Playing pranks on furry friends.

A caterpillar wears a hat,
While ants debate where they're at.
A ladybug starts a band,
With a rhythm that's quite unplanned.

The rabbits hop in synchronized bliss,
Thinking they're stars in a ballet twist.
Every twig has a tale to spin,
Of the laughter that bubbles within.

With petals that tickle and tease,
Nature's humor flows with ease.
In this carnival of the green,
Life's punchlines are fit for a queen.

Nature's Gentle Patina

In the woods where giggles float,
Mushrooms don their finest coat.
A hedgehog snickers, quite the sight,
As a beetle steals the spotlight.

The flowers gossip, petals in a swirl,
"Did you see how that snail gave a twirl?"
A butterfly whispers, "Well, I'd like to try,"
As it flutters past, waving goodbye.

Branches sway with playful intent,
As squirrels scheme with crumbs they've lent.
Caterpillars curl up for a nap,
Dreaming of an upcoming trap.

In this quirky, quiet scene,
Nature's jesters reign supreme.
And as the sun begins to dip,
The laughter echoes, a joyous trip.

Luminescence in the Lowlands

Where twinkling lights dance in the night,
A firefly flicks on its flight.
In the grass, the critters plot,
As crickets provide the comical lot.

A frog in his finest bow tie,
Croaking tunes to the evening sky.
Worms do the twist in dirt below,
Calling all friends to join the show.

Shimmering dew drops, a glimmering throne,
As the moon hums a playful drone.
Each corner sings a funny refrain,
In the lowlands, joy runs like rain.

So come take a peek at wonders rare,
In nature's theater, laughter's in the air.
With each blink and flutter in sight,
We find our giggles light as night.

Reflections of the Earth's Canvas

In the garden, green fluff grows,
Fashioned hats for the frogs' shows.
They croak in rhythm, dressed to impress,
All while dodging a snake in a mess.

Sprouting humor in patches quite rare,
The snails host races, without a care.
Their tiny shells shiny and bright,
As they slide into the garden night.

The beetles play chess on a leaf,
While ants perform their dance, no grief.
A bug symphony fills the air,
Eager to win a dance-off fair.

Nature's laughter fills the ground,
Where whimsy and wonder abound.
In every nook, each crevice and crack,
Life's comedy waits, never to lack.

The Language of Silent Growth

Underneath the soil, secrets are stored,
The roots gather round, ready to hoard.
They gossip in whispers, a tale of delight,
As worms wiggle through in the moonlight.

A wandering dandelion chose her fate,
Declared herself queen, but it's running late.
With petals like crowns, she puffs and sighs,
Swaying gently as the wind flies.

The shy mushrooms peep, with spots like confetti,
Cracking jokes while staying quite petty.
In their tiny circles, they brew their tea,
With laughter that's caught by the curious bee.

And when dawn breaks, it's a waltz on the grass,
Each blade like a dancer, they move with sass.
In the hush of the morn, chortles ensue,
As the sun gives a wink, just for the crew.

Echoing in the Underbrush

In the thicket, a chatter ignites,
Hedgehogs in coats of fashion that excites.
They roll and they tumble, a party of spines,
While squirrels tell tales of grand acorns' fines.

The bushes are crowded with banter and cheer,
As chipmunks recount how they conquered fear.
With each little tumble, a hiccup rings true,
Nature's giggles echo, fresh morning dew.

A pair of rabbits engage in a race,
With floppy ears flapping, they pick up the pace.
Not far behind, a tortoise takes note,
Sipping tea while time goes afloat.

And when twilight descends, the critters convene,
Reciting their tales and their dreams of the green.
With laughter as soft as the stars up above,
The underbrush whispers, a frolicsome love.

A Verse of Verdant Thoughts

In the thickets where laughter entwines with the air,
Frogs crack wise, without a care.
They sing silly songs in a concert of croaks,
As fireflies burst in the night with their jokes.

A patch of ferns holds a secret or two,
They snicker at grass, always newbie to dew.
The elder twigs share wisdom uncouth,
While the younger sprouts seek the fountain of truth.

The blanket of leaves has a rhythm divine,
And in its sweet rustle, the secrets entwine.
Each creature a bard, creating a scene,
Telling tall tales of the spaces between.

With giggles of petals in the warm summer light,
The woods come alive in the embrace of the night.
From roots to the sky, mischief abounds,
In this playful sanctuary, joy knows no bounds.

A Spectrum of Green

In a forest, under leaves,
I found a patch that believes.
It tickles toes, oh what a show,
Fluffy carpets where the wild things grow.

A frog leaps high, then lands with splats,
He thinks he's grand in his green habitat.
Try to catch him, if you dare,
But be ready for mud, just beware!

The snails parade with slimy grace,
While worms wiggle in this happy place.
Dancing beetles join the scene,
What a riot in this shade of green!

So next time you wander, just take a peek,
In funny splendor, nature's cheek.
A world where laughter spins and plays,
Amidst the greens of sunny days.

Beneath the Boughs

Beneath the boughs, where shadows hide,
Squirrels chatter, full of pride.
They store their snacks for winter's chill,
Counting acorns, what a thrill!

A raccoon snickers at my feet,
Daring me to join his feat.
Climbing trees and eating fries,
In his world, no one complies!

The owls are hooting their own tune,
While chipmunks dance beneath the moon.
As they trip over twigs, oh dear!
It's a circus show, come grab a seat here!

So laugh along with nature's play,
In the forest, fun's the only way.
Just remember to wear your shoes,
Adventure lies in every ooze.

Reflections in the dampness

In puddles deep, the sky peeks down,
Fluffy clouds wear a watery crown.
Sipping rain, a joyful jest,
Nature laughs, it knows what's best.

A duck with style, struts about,
Quacking jokes, he has no doubt.
With webbed feet flapping in the breeze,
He's the king of mockery, if you please!

The frogs are croaking their own song,
Each one thinks it won't be long.
For one to hop upon a star,
Then plop back down—how bizarre!

So gaze into the gleaming wet,
Where silly thoughts and puddles met.
Life's just a splash, a funny chase,
In every drop, there's joy and grace.

Delicate Layers of Life

Beneath the layers soft and light,
Creatures dance in pure delight.
Ants parade with tunes to share,
While spiders weave without a care.

A ladybug rolls in the grime,
She thinks she's fancy, how sublime!
With polka dots and tiny wings,
She tells the world the joy it brings!

Worms wiggle down, their party's tight,
Dirt-colored friends in work's delight.
They dig and twist, quite unashamed,
Turning soil, yet never blamed.

So prance along in life's embrace,
In every nook, find happy space.
Embrace the quirks, the giggles rife,
In delicate layers, discover life!

Whispers Beneath the Canopy

In shadows deep, the squirrels play,
They gossip loud, but fade away.
With acorns dropped and twigs that snap,
A chatty world in nature's lap.

The branches sway, a secret dance,
While bamboo whispers make us glance.
A rabbit hops, a leafy sight,
And winks at us, all in good night.

Green Enchantment of the Forest Floor

Among the ferns, a debate takes flight,
A snail is slow, but claims he's bright.
The beetles race, they're quite a crew,
While fungi giggle in shades of blue.

The shadows play, the colors blend,
With each green hue, the laughter sends.
A turtle slow, a hare in rush,
Who'll win the game? Oh, what a hush!

Soft Shadows of Ancient Pines

Beneath the pines, the shadows stretch,
Where chubby chipmunks try to fetch.
They climb up high to grab a nut,
Then tumble down with quite a thud.

The whispers swirl, a breeze of jest,
Each little creature knows the best.
While pine cones drop with goofy plops,
A laughter chorus never stops.

Lichen Lullabies in the Dappled Light

A lizard sings a tune so sweet,
While slugs keep time on tiny feet.
The sunbeams dance on leafy beds,
With dreamy thoughts that fill our heads.

The creeping vines engage in play,
As shadows shift and drift away.
In dappled light, it's plain to see,
Nature's fun is wild and free.

Veil of Verdant Dreams

Beneath the leaves, a squirrel leaps,
Twirling around, in silence it creeps.
With acorns stashed, it strikes a pose,
Winks at the world, then off it goes.

A frog in the pond sings opera loud,
While dragonflies dance, a wobbly crowd.
The humor hides in every nook,
Nature's own tale, just open the book.

A snail slides by, wearing its home,
Chasing its dream in a leafy dome.
With trails like art, its path is a treat,
Slow and steady, it won't miss a beat.

So lift your cup, tea or some cheer,
Nature's a stand-up, with jokes to share.
In leafy laughter, life's quite a show,
Who knew green could steal the glow?

Underfoot Reveries in the Wet Earth

In the garden, worms dig a groove,
Twirling their tails, they're on the move.
A puddle reflects a marshy mirth,
Splashing the sky, oh what a birth!

A beetle rolls by in a shiny ball,
Thinks it's a race, decides to stall.
Why rush through life, when you can roll?
Every clump of dirt makes it feel whole.

When raindrops fall, a parade begins,
Each one a dancer, in gleeful spins.
They wear tiny hats, so debonair,
Laughing at flowers, unkempt and rare.

The earth beneath wiggles with glee,
Plenty of giggles, so carefree.
So next time you step, give a little cheer,
For the silly lives, we adore, my dear!

Ferns Cradle Thoughts in Stillness

Ferns whisper secrets in the faint breeze,
Telling the tales with a rustle of leaves.
A caterpillar passed with a sigh,
"Why rush to be great? Just munch and fly!"

Under the boughs, the shadows play,
Tickling the nosy ants on their way.
They march like soldiers, in single file,
Searching for crumbs, they travel in style.

A lizard looks on, flashes a grin,
Who knew that a bug could wear such a skin?
With twitchy tales and eyes that blink,
He plots his next move in a steady wink.

So linger a while, let your thoughts flow,
Amongst leafy giants and funny shows.
In the tranquility, find all that gleams,
Nature's foolery fills up our dreams!

Hidden Stories in the Shade

In the shadows, stories intertwine,
A sleepy mouse finds a path so fine.
Dreams of cheese float through its mind,
"Today, I'll feast, my luck will unwind!"

Then, a bunny hops, with a twist and a twirl,
Dancing like nobody, giving a whirl.
"What a life!" it chirps, quite proud of the day,"
While chasing its tail in a humorous way.

The sunbeams flicker, casting some light,
A slug thinks it's winning this silly fight.
With a grin and a wiggle, it glides along,
Singing a tune, quite the charming song!

So gather your thoughts in the dappled shade,
Among the odd critters that dance and parade.
Life's a circus, in this leafy dome,
Laugh a little louder, it's a magical home!

Serenity in the Softness

In the garden, soft and round,
A green delight upon the ground.
I trip and tumble, oh what fun,
This airy dance with nature's sun.

A frog leaps by, a sudden splash,
Startles me as I start to dash.
With giggles loud, I find my place,
In the cozy, squishy embrace.

The rain drops down in playful rounds,
And joins the party on the grounds.
Each droplet sings, a jolly cheer,
While ants parade, my laughter near.

So here I sit, a child once more,
Exploring secrets on the floor.
With every whisper, soft and sly,
Nature chuckles, oh my, oh my!

Forgotten Realms of the Earth Below

Beneath the roots, a world so grand,
With critters plotting, oh so planned.
A colony with snacks galore,
While I just wonder, what's in store?

The worms have gathered, what a scene,
Discussing dirt, oh what's their theme?
They wiggle tales of mischief done,
Sprinkling humor, just for fun!

The beetles boast of battles fought,
While ants debate the best of snot.
I laugh out loud, they turn to me,
Who knew earth's floor held comedy?

In this kingdom where I peek,
Their humor's sharp, their banter cheek.
Among the roots, I find my place,
In laughter's arms, a warm embrace!

Reflections on a Cushion of Green

Upon a patch, I plop right down,
Surveying all, the greenish crown.
The dandelions wink and tease,
While butterflies float on the breeze.

A squirrel scampers, tail held high,
With acorn jokes that make me sigh.
He chases shadows, leaps with flair,
While I'm entranced by his wild hair.

The soft ground beckons me to stay,
As clouds drift by, it seems to play.
A picnic here beneath the trees,
With nature's laughter in the breeze.

So here I lay, a thoughtless soul,
With giggles bubbling, feeling whole.
In a sea of green, the world feels right,
We share this cheer, oh what a sight!

The Language of Leafy Silence

Among the branches, whispers float,
Each leaf a secret, each tree a note.
I pause to listen, what do they say?
In leafy silence, they joke and play.

The breeze brings whispers, soft and light,
A chuckle travels, a giggle takes flight.
As branches sway, they trade their puns,
While critters dance, oh what fun runs!

A lazy cat, with eyes so wide,
Joins in the laughter, there's nothing to hide.
In this leafy chat, I find great glee,
For nature's humor is wild and free.

So I rejoice in this forest fair,
With every chuckle curling in the air.
In the stillness, joy takes root,
With leafy laughter, my heart's resolute!

Echoes of the Sylvan Silence

In a forest deep, where whispers play,
The squirrels debate, in their own nutty way.
Trees lean in close, eavesdropping keen,
Laughing at owls, who think they are seen.

A rabbit hops by, with ears in a twist,
Wondering how it came to exist.
While chipmunks giggle, in their tiny attire,
Plotting a scheme to steal acorns from higher.

The Comfort of Nature's Carpet

Underfoot lies a cushion soft and green,
Where every step feels like a dance, so serene.
The bugs join in, with a patter and hum,
While ants march along, humming 'Here we come!'

A picnic of petals, where daisies do bloom,
Yelling, 'Here we are, in the great outdoors room!'
And frogs serenade, with their froggy croaks,
In a waltz with the bees, in a world full of jokes.

Gentle Hesitations in the Wilderness

A turtle takes pause, pondering the sun,
While birds laugh around, having just begun.
With a wiggle of toes, the hare makes a dash,
While a sloth in the corner has a leisurely splash.

The wise old turtle moans, 'Why rush through the day?
When flowers hold secrets they dare not say?'
And butterflies flutter, with a wink and a toss,
Making the hare realize it's a race he might lose.

Emerald Thoughts on a Rainy Day

Puddles reflect a world upside down,
Where frogs hold court, and they wear a crown.
Raindrops tap dance, on leaves big and small,
While worms wiggle out, catching the call.

A bear with an umbrella prepares for a swim,
While the insects gather, singing on a whim.
Laughter echoes, as lightning strikes bold,
In a realm where the wild knows no chill, just gold.

Secrets of the Earth's Palms

In the garden, secrets hide,
You'd think they'd run and glide.
But there they sit, all slick and bold,
The tales they tell, never old.

A cheeky worm may crack a grin,
While thinking of the life within.
A dancing beetle joins the show,
With tiny boots and quite a flow.

They scheme beneath the leafy throne,
Spying on us, all alone.
Do they gossip like we do?
Or maybe start a wormy brew?

So here's a toast to nature's glee,
To all the critters, wild and free.
For every tuft and blade that sways,
Holds all their secrets, in kooky ways.

Silent Soliloquies of Nature

Amidst the leaves, a whisper lay,
With dappled light, it comes to play.
The squirrels chuckle, tails on high,
In dialogues that make you sigh.

A snail once claimed to rule the night,
But slipped on dew, oh what a fright!
While crickets laugh, they sing out loud,
To all the bugs, a lively crowd.

Leaves rustle with a wink and nod,
While ants parade, with tiny sod.
They march in lines, a neat little troop,
Leading each other to food or a loop.

And if you listen, you might hear,
The stories spun through laughter near.
In nature's realm, all are bemused,
With every sound, our hearts infused.

The Soft Embrace of Time

Time wraps us in a leafy hug,
With sleepy stems and a cozy bug.
The shadows dance, like soft whispers,
While moments glide, like fleeting twisters.

A pebble grins beneath a shoe,
Like 'Hey! Where'd you get that view?'
The sun peeks in, with a bright salute,
While daisies nod in cute pursuit.

Each tick of clocks in nature's hand,
Holds tiny tales of a seasoned band.
While an old oak chuckles, wise and grand,
With roots that know this magic land.

In this embrace, we stop to ponder,
Lost in joy, we happily wander.
For time may stretch like a slimy vine,
In the garden where our dreams entwine.

Underfoot Enigmas

Beneath our feet, a world unfolds,
With secrets shy, and stories bold.
The grass giggles when we walk,
In whispers shared, they softly talk.

A toadstool rolls its eyes, how rude!
As raindrops plop in jubilant dude.
Caterpillars munch without a care,
While crickets plot urban flair.

Each footstep stirs a hidden laugh,
A riddle wrapped in greenish craft.
The earth beneath, with subtle flair,
Calls out to those who wish to share.

So tread with glee on this soft bed,
Where oddities lie and wonders spread.
For every stumble, giggle, or fall,
Reveals the magic, under it all.

Nature's Textured Thoughts

In the woods where silence snores,
Life teems through ancient floors.
A squirrel's got a secret stash,
He'll share it if you bring some trash.

A slug's on a quest for a snack,
Wonders where the lettuce's at.
Why do snails race in slow-mo?
Maybe it's a secret show!

The trees gossip in their green lace,
They giggle at the human race.
Whispers through the boughs and sighs,
They chuckle as the owl flies by.

The fungi wear a funny cap,
Like they're setting up a trap.
In this realm of oddball cheer,
Who knew nature had a sense of queer?

The Beauty of Slow Growth

A sprout's in no urgent race,
Just stretching out to find its space.
It checked its watch and thought, why fuss?
When being still is quite a plus?

An acorn dreams of mighty trees,
While dodging all the squirrel's pleas.
It's taking notes on rustling leaves,
Learning life in less than eves.

The patience game is hard to win,
But the tortoise learned to grin.
As flowers burst in color's strife,
They joke about the "fast track" life.

The roots all hold a secret sale,
"Buy two, get growth!" they laugh and wail.
In patience, humor finds a home,
With plants that stretch but rarely roam.

Enigmas of the Forest's Embrace

Under branches, mysteries dwell,
Where every fungal hat blends well.
The bushes giggle, hiding spots,
While creatures laugh at tangled knots.

Why do the crickets sing at night?
Is it an ode to snack on plight?
A rabbit scoffs, 'That's just for fun!'
As he hops under the setting sun.

A fox once wore a leafy crown,
Claiming it the best in town.
The other critters rolled their eyes,
While judging fashion in disguise.

Secrets linger in the shade,
Like treasure chests by nature made.
Who knew that all the greens could wink?
Their only rule? Well, just don't blink.

Creep of the Quiet Green

Creeping slowly, the shadows grin,
Play hide-and-seek with a sneaky bin.
A patch of green stole the show,
As a deer danced around in a flow.

The carpet whispers stories old,
Of mossy knights and tales retold.
'What time is it?' a beetle asks,
As he polishes his shiny tasks.

Hidden critters plot and plan,
On leaves that hold a secret span.
The creeping charm of quiet thrills,
Like unexpected nature drills.

With every twist and every turn,
Nature's got a laugh to earn.
So step lightly, join the jive,
In this green world, we all revive.

Green Velvet Dreams

In the garden where gizmos dwell,
Fuzzy green hats wear secrets well.
Whispers of snails trail all around,
Jokes in the shade, laughter unbound.

A worm in a top hat, quite the sight,
Dancing with daisies, oh what a night!
Grass blades like swords in a playful duel,
Nature's own jesters, breaking the rule.

Crickets wear ties, the fireflies glow,
Party on petals, with glitter in tow.
Bumbles in bowties zip through the fair,
Crowned by the sun, they float in midair.

A tickle of breeze makes the daisies chuckle,
Nature's own stand-up, optional buckle.
Laughter abounds on the velvet green bed,
Dreams topped with giggles, all worries shed.

Secrets of the Shaded Floor

Under the canopy, chatter ignites,
Squirrels in sequins, oh what delights!
Willow trees giggle, a hidden scene,
While critters plot mischief, sly and mean.

A hedgehog in spectacles, reading a book,
Gives life advice with a wise little look.
Ants in a chorus, their voices combine,
Singing their anthem, oh how they shine!

Frogs throw a party, no toads allowed,
Jumping in harmony, making it loud.
The secrets unfold on the shaded floor,
Where laughter and antics are hard to ignore.

Mice on a tightrope, oh they perform,
Cheese in the crowd, their snacks now the norm.
In this playful theater, fun reigns supreme,
Nature's own circus, living the dream.

Echoes in Emerald Shadows

In the twilight glow, shadows collide,
Chirps and chuckles, nature's best guide.
Beneath leafy arches, tales start to spin,
Laughter erupts where the fun has been.

A raccoon in boots, so stylish and sly,
Shimmies and shakes, oh my, oh my!
Sipping sweet nectar, bees have a ball,
While ants in tuxedos waltz down the hall.

Ferns whisper secrets, giggling in green,
Echoes of nonsense, the best ever seen.
Freckles of sunlight dance on the ground,
As chuckles and chatter grow ever profound.

The moon, a spotlighter, beams down with glee,
While creatures unveil their wild jubilee.
In these rich shadows, life takes a chance,
Bursting with laughter, the world starts to dance.

Fables of the Forest Floor

Tales from the roots where the stories are spun,
Fables of frolic, and mischief for fun.
Hares in high hats offer life's best advice,
While foxes scribble when fortune seems nice.

A tortoise with swagger steps into view,
Challenging rabbits, saying, "Just watch what I do!"
While squirrels collect hats, their treasure so grand,
Sprinting with giggles, not quite what they planned.

Mushrooms in circles hold midnight tea,
Frogs croak in harmony, sing merrily.
Fireflies twinkle, like stars that have fled,
Lighting the path where fun never dread.

The forest is buzzin', with tales never bore,
Laughter and stories, forever the score.
Nature's own fables, where joy's always core,
Echoes and giggles from the forest floor.

The Earth's Quiet Narratives

In the garden, secrets hide,
A worm wears glasses, full of pride.
A pebble tells tales, big and small,
While ants march on like they own it all.

A snail's slow dance, quite the affair,
He stops for tea, if you can spare.
The daisies giggle, watch him slip,
As clovers plot a mischief trip!

Beneath Feet and Ferns

Underfoot, a critter's race,
An ant with shades, a tiny face.
A leaf whispers jokes, such a tease,
While beetles join in with ease.

The grass blades critique every step,
As frogs croak puns, a comic rep.
Watch where you tread, it's a riot here,
Nature's jesters, no doubt, my dear!

Textures of Tranquility

A carpet green, woven tight,
Tickling toes, pure delight.
Fungi gather, a party dare,
Sipping dew in the sunlit air.

The rocks play chess, with leaves as pawns,
While crickets strum their twilight songs.
Each nook holds laughter, stirs delight,
In this haven, everything's right!

Of Roots and Reflections

Roots beneath, a tangled mess,
Whispers of jokes that they confess.
A squirrel's grin, a nut in tow,
Stopped for laughter, oh what a show!

Water droplets, crystal clear,
Riptide gags for all to hear.
Life dances low, dreams rise high,
Join the revelry, don't be shy!

Conversations with the Underworld

In the shadows, whispers creep,
Chortling gnomes, oh, what a heap!
They trade tales of lost shoes,
And snack on the morning dew.

Beneath the root, a laughter churns,
A silly dance as daylight burns.
Spiders spin a web so fine,
As they sip on elderflower wine.

With worms discussing their next meal,
They chuckle loud, it's quite the deal.
Raccoons join, with bandit masks,
Exchanging secrets in cozy tasks.

But hush now, keep the volume low,
For even ghosts don't want to know.
When roots gather 'round for a chat,
You best be ready for a whimsy spat.

Footfalls through Ferns

Step lightly where the ferns do sway,
A hidden path leads the curious astray.
Giggling frogs and their fine attire,
A hop, a leap—oh, joyous choir!

A snail in a hurry, what a treat,
With a trail of slime, can't be beat!
They ponder the meaning of life's great race,
While pondering pudding, at their own pace.

Beneath a leaf, a committee meets,
Debating the merits of leftover beets.
A ladybug dons a tiny crown,
Proclaiming the day, she won't back down!

As the sun dips low, the chatter grows,
Of lost socks and shoes that no one knows.
With laughter echoing through the glade,
Here in the wild, all joy is made.

Enchantment of the Earthly Green

Among the green, where nonsense thrives,
The ants host parties, and fungus jives.
A squirrel debates, with a pinecone, too,
Should they wear socks, red or blue?

Dancing daisies twirl in the breeze,
Whispering secrets, teasing the trees.
A clumsy beetle trips over moss,
Declares it chic, though at quite a loss.

In the shade, a raccoon gives a wink,
While pondering if he should learn to blink.
With chipmunks gathering tales of the day,
They plot their antics, come what may.

The sun sets slow, the night takes hold,
Their stories weave, silly and bold.
In this verdant realm where friendships gleam,
Life's a giggle, or so it seems.

The Haiku of Hidden Growth

Underneath the stone,
Tiny beings plot their fun,
Laughter in the roots.

Greens whisper soft jokes,
A flower hides, laughs repeat,
Wonders in the shade.

Ants march with a flair,
In a conga line, they dare,
To challenge the wind.

Life rolls like a ball,
Silly songs from every leaf,
Jubilant and free.

www.ingramcontent.com/pod-product-compliance
Lightning Source LLC
Chambersburg PA
CBHW072148200426
43209CB00051B/864